SCHOLASTIC

GRADES 2–3

Reading Response Trifolds for 40 Favorite Chapter Books

Reproducible Independent Reading Management Tools That Guide Students to Use Essential Reading Strategies and Respond Meaningfully to Literature

by Jennifer Cerra-Johansson

New York • Toronto • London • Auckland • Sydney
Mexico City • New Delhi • Hong Kong • Buenos Aires

Teaching *Resources*

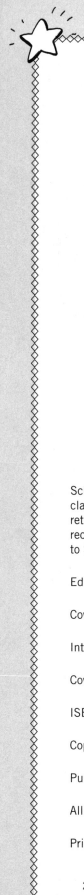

For Lukas, Will, and Ella—my three favorite bookworms

Edited by Mela Ottaiano

Cover design by Wendy Chan

Interior design by Melinda Belter

Cover and interior illustrations by Teresa Anderko

ISBN: 978-0-545-30554-9

Copyright © 2011 by Jennifer Cerra-Johansson

Published by Scholastic Inc.

Printed in the U.S.A.

2 3 4 5 6 7 8 9 10   40   17 16 15 14 13 12 11

Contents

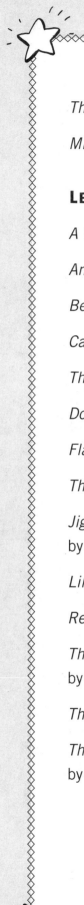

Level O

Level P

Level Q

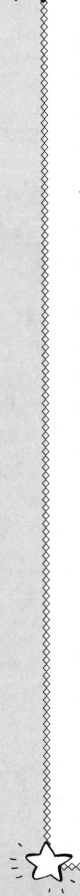
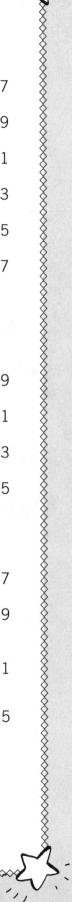

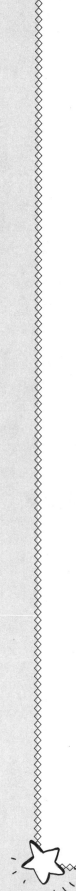

Introduction

As an elementary school teacher, I strive to instill a love of reading in my students. To do this, I explicitly teach reading skills and strategies through guided reading so students are *able* to read. I also carefully choose books that students will *want* to read.

Because one of my goals is to help students see reading as a fun activity rather than a chore, I make it a point to select high-interest chapter books I'm sure they will enjoy. (For instance, the first book in a series will typically "hook" students, so I often choose these, leading them to read the other books in the series during independent reading time.) Once I've chosen a book, the next step is to read it critically and identify the reading strategies I want students to apply. Even though chapter books at these grade levels aren't necessarily very long, this process can still be time consuming. As I work, I keep in mind the importance of helping my students purposefully read and remain focused. I also want to hold them accountable for what they read and to easily assess their understanding and progress—while having several groups read different chapter books simultaneously. To help me accomplish all this, I use reading response trifolds specific to each chapter book as part of my guided-reading instruction.

What Are Reading Response Trifolds?

Reading response trifolds are activity sheets that students refer to and interact with during each guided-reading session. Students can also use the folded sheet as a convenient bookmark. Each trifold contains three parts: Strategy, Focus, and Respond. The *Strategy* component helps students review a specific reading comprehension strategy, such as predicting, making connections, or using context clues. Next students read the *Focus* section, where they are given a purpose for reading a specific section of the text. After students have finished reading the entire section, they answer the *Respond* question. This requires them to refer back to the reading and apply the specific reading strategy to formulate their response.

Trifolds in Action

Using trifolds as part of my guided-reading instruction has proven to be an effective way to teach and reinforce reading strategies. To introduce or review a particular section's strategy, I begin by asking students to tell me what they know or remember about the strategy. I follow up this discussion with a "think-aloud," where I read from a text, apply the strategy, and share my thought process out loud. This model provides students with an internal dialogue they can apply when reading independently.

You might say the following when doing a think-aloud for each strategy:

According to Fountas and Pinnell's guided-reading text gradient, second graders typically read between levels H–M, and third graders range from level L–P. Once students can read at level K, their decoding skills are advanced enough that more emphasis can be place on higher level reading strategies and responses. We included books through level Q to provide material for more advanced third grade readers.

Predict

- What do you think will happen if _____?
- What do you think will happen next?
- I think the character will _____.
- How do you think the story might end?

Question

- Why did the author include this section?
- Why did the character do that?
- Why did that happen?

Make Inferences

- What do you think the character meant?
- Why did he/she do that?
- What does this show us?
- How does the character feel?

Find the Main Idea

- What was the most important part?
- What key event or events stand out in your mind?
- Why is the chapter title a good one for this chapter?

Evaluate

- What did you like or dislike?
- How did you feel as you read?
- What was your favorite/least favorite part?
- Do you agree with _____ ?
- What lesson did you learn from the story?

Visualize

- What did you see in your mind as you read?
- How did you picture the character?
- What do you imagine the setting looked like?
- What do these details show?

Analyze Cause and Effect

- How did the characters affect each other?
- How did a character's actions affect the story events?
- How might things have turned out differently if _____?

Make Connections

- What does this story/event/part remind you of?
- When have you had a similar experience?
- Have you ever felt this way?
- Does this character remind you of someone you know?
- Have you ever been to a place like this?

Use Context Clues

- What other word would make sense here?
- What clues do you see in the sentence?
- What might this mean?

After going over a reading strategy, we continue by previewing the *Focus* question in the same section. Students then read a small amount of the text, keeping that question in mind. While students read silently, I spend a few minutes with each student, listening to them read aloud. This enables me to help students improve their fluency, expression, and decoding skills.

Once students have finished reading the entire section and have answered the *Respond* section independently, they share their responses with the group. As they share, I can assess their understanding of the material, and students can work through any confusion on the spot.

The trifolds serve as both an instructional tool and a management technique. I generally have four or five different guided-reading groups going in my classroom each day—using four or five different books. Remembering specific story events and which strategies would best suit a section of text can be challenging without a system in place. Preparing these trifolds ahead of time consistently helps my guided-reading groups run smoothly and efficiently. Using them has enabled me to meet the diverse needs of my students. Children love guided-reading time because they have the opportunity to read quality literature at their independent reading levels, and interact with the text and the teacher.

Using the trifolds in the context of guided reading offers students a smooth transition to using them during independent reading—enhancing their experience and developing a joy of reading.

 To identify the editions that were used to create these trifold assignments, please refer to the bibliography on page 95. While the use of page numbers has been kept to a minimum, it was necessary to identify certain passages. If you are using a different edition than the one in the bibliography, please preview the sheet before distributing it to students. The page numbers may not be off by very much, and you should only need a quick scan of the material to make any necessary revisions. If you do need to revise the page numbers, you may want to photocopy one trifold first. Then you can use correcting liquid to cover the old page numbers and write in those that match the edition you are using.

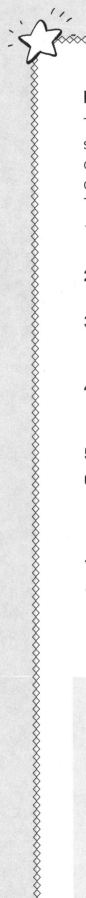

How to Assemble a Trifold

To assemble the reading response trifolds so they appear back-to-back (as they do in the book), you'll need access to a copier that makes double-sided copies. Then, follow these easy steps:

figure 1

1. Make single-sided photocopies of both trifold pages. (See figure 1.)

2. Place one page on top of the other. They should both be facing up.

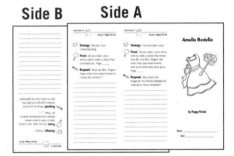

figure 2

3. Flip one of the pages so that the pages are oriented in opposite directions. (See figure 2.)

4. Feed pages through a photocopier set to create 1 double-sided page from 2 single-sided pages.

5. Distribute a trifold sheet to each student.

6. Direct them to place the side with the title panel facedown. Then they should fold the panels so that the title page ends up on top, similar to a brochure. (See figure 3.)

figure 3

7. Finally, have students follow the directions on each of the panels to complete the reading response trifolds. If students find they need more room to write or to illustrate, they can use a separate sheet of paper and attach it to the trifold with a stapler.

TIP If you don't have access to a copier that makes double-sided copies, you can glue or staple the pages back to back before distributing them to students. (See figures 4 and 5.) Then students can continue directly to steps 6 and 7.

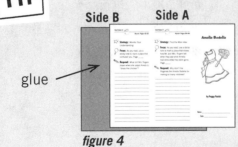

glue

figure 4

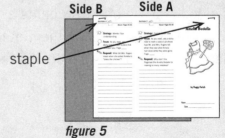

staple

figure 5

Mercy Watson to the Rescue

by Kate DiCamillo

Name _____

Date _____

SECTION 5   **READ:** Chapters 10–12

Strategy: Evaluate

Focus: As you read, use a sticky note to mark where Mercy gets a reward. Page _____

Respond: Do you think Mercy is a hero? Why or why not?

SECTION 4   **READ:** Chapters 7–9

Strategy: Find the Main Idea

Focus: As you read, use a sticky note to mark where someone comes to help the Watsons. Page _____

Respond: Who do the Watsons think called the fire department? Why?

⭐ **Strategy:** Predict

🔍 **Focus:** Based on the cover, title, and illustrations, predict what you think might happen in the story.

✏️ **Respond:** As the Watsons and Mercy were sleeping, the floor moaned and the bed cracked. Predict what you think will happen next.

_____
_____
_____
_____
_____
_____
_____
_____
_____

⭐ **Strategy:** Question

🔍 **Focus:** As you read Chapter 3, use a sticky note to mark where the Watsons encounter a problem. Page _____

✏️ **Respond:** Why doesn't Mercy go for help?

_____
_____
_____
_____
_____
_____
_____
_____

⭐ **Strategy:** Make Inferences

🔍 **Focus:** As you read Chapter 5, use a sticky note to mark where Mercy causes another problem. Page _____

✏️ **Respond:** On page 37, Baby says, "Oh dear." How is she feeling on this page? Why is she feeling this way?

_____
_____
_____
_____
_____
_____
_____

Amelia Bedelia

by Peggy Parish

Name _____

Date _____

SECTION 5

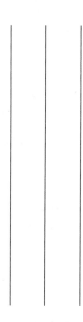

READ: Pages 54–64

 Strategy: Find the Main Idea

 **Focus:** As you read, use a sticky note to mark a place that shows how Mr. and Mrs. Rogers felt when they saw what Amelia had done while they were gone. Page _____

Respond: Why didn't Mr. and Mrs. Rogers fire Amelia Bedelia for making so many mistakes?

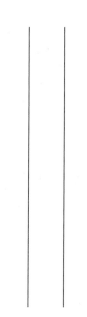

SECTION 4

READ: Pages 42–53

Strategy: Monitor Your Understanding

 Focus: As you read, use a sticky note to mark a place that confused you. Page _____

 Respond: What did Mrs. Rogers mean when she asked Amelia to "dress the chicken"?

★ **Strategy:** Question

 Focus: Flip through the first few pages of the story. Write one question that came to your mind.

 Respond: What is Amelia Bedelia's new job?

_____

Was your question answered by the end of today's reading?

_____

★ **Strategy:** Make Inferences

 Focus: As you read, use a sticky note to mark a place where Amelia does something silly. Page ____

Respond: When Mrs. Rogers wrote that Amelia should "draw the drapes," what did she want Amelia to do?

_____

★ **Strategy:** Predict

 Focus: As you read, use a sticky note to mark a place where Amelia misunderstands what to do. Page ____

Respond: What do you think Amelia is going to do with the bits of ribbon she has gathered?

_____

Cam Jansen and the Mystery of the Stolen Diamonds

by **David A. Adler**

Name _____

Date _____

 **READ: Chapters 7 and 8**

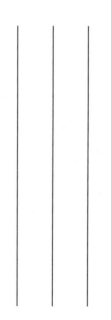 **Strategy:** Make Inferences

Focus: As you read Chapter 7, use a sticky note to mark the place where Cam has an idea and solves a problem. Page _____

Respond: Why did Cam, Eric, and the policeman laugh on the last page of Chapter 8?

_____

_____

_____

_____

_____

_____

 READ: Chapter 6

  **Strategy:** Visualize

Focus: As you read, use a sticky note to mark a place you could visualize well. Page _____

Respond: Reread the bottom of page 48. Draw a picture of what you visualized.

READ: Chapter 1

Strategy: Predict

Focus: As you read, use a sticky note to mark a place where you learn something important about Cam. Page ____

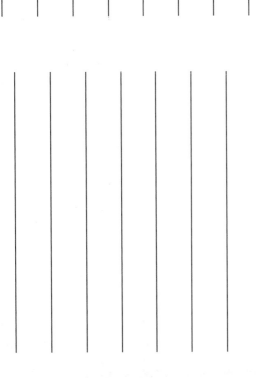

Respond: Predict why you think the man ran out of the store so quickly.

_____
_____
_____
_____
_____
_____
_____
_____
_____
_____

READ: Chapters 2 and 3

Strategy: Find the Main Idea

Focus: As you read Chapter 2, use a sticky note to mark the place where you discover what happened in the jewelry store. Page ____

Respond: What surprised you on the last page of Chapter 3?

_____
_____
_____
_____
_____
_____
_____
_____
_____
_____

READ: Chapters 4 and 5

Strategy: Question

Focus: As you read Chapter 4, use a sticky note to mark the place where Cam realizes something strange is going on. Page ____

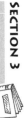

Respond: Why did the man and woman bring a baby into the jewelry store?

_____
_____
_____
_____
_____
_____
_____
_____
_____
_____

The Cobble Street Cousins: In Aunt Lucy's Kitchen

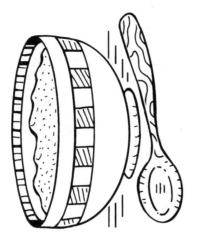

by Cynthia Rylant

Name _____

Date _____

SECTION 5   AFTER READING

Strategy: Make Connections

Respond: If you could create your own kind of company, what kind would you create? Why?

_____
_____
_____
_____
_____
_____
_____
_____
_____
_____

SECTION 4

READ: Chapter 3 "The Show"

Strategy: Analyze Cause and Effect

Focus: As you read, use a sticky note to mark where a character feels happy. Page _____

Respond: How did the cookie company affect the characters in the story?

_____
_____
_____
_____
_____
_____
_____
_____

☆ **Strategy:** Question

🔍 **Focus:** Look at the cover, title, and illustrations. Before reading the story, write two questions that came to your mind. As you read, see if your questions are answered.

Q: _____

_____

A: _____

_____

Q: _____

_____

A: _____

_____

☆ **Strategy:** Evaluate

🔍 **Focus:** As you read, use a sticky note to mark where you learn Lily's idea. Page ____

✏️ **Respond:** What is Lily's idea? Do you think it's a good idea? Why or why not?

_____

_____

_____

_____

☆ **Strategy:** Find the Main Idea

🔍 **Focus:** As you read, use a sticky note to mark where the girls do something kind. Page ____

✏️ **Respond:** How did the girls feel about making the cookie deliveries? Why did they feel this way?

_____

_____

_____

_____

Horrible Harry
in
Room 2B

2 B

by Suzy Kline

Name _____

Date _____

READ: Chapter 5
"Horrible Harry and the
Field Trip"

Strategy: Evaluate

Focus: As you read, use a sticky note to mark a place where Harry makes a bad decision.
Page _____

Respond: Would you want to be Harry's friend? Why or why not?

_____
_____
_____
_____
_____
_____
_____
_____
_____

READ: Chapter 4
"Horrible Harry and the
Thanksgiving Play"

Strategy: Make Inferences

Focus: As you read, use a sticky note to mark where Harry does something kind. Page _____

Respond: Reread page 40. What do you think Harry says to Song Lee's mother on the phone?

_____
_____
_____
_____
_____
_____
_____
_____
_____

READ: Chapter 1
"Horrible Harry and Me"

☆ **Strategy:** Predict

 Focus: Who do you think will tell the story?

 Respond: Do you think Doug and Harry will stay best friends? Why or why not?

As you read, use a sticky note to mark the place where you find out. Page _____

_____

_____

_____

_____

_____

_____

_____

READ: Chapter 2
"Horrible Harry, the Stub People, and Halloween"

☆ **Strategy:** Question

 Focus: As you read, use a sticky note to mark where Harry's plan fails. Page _____

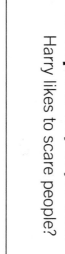 **Respond:** Why do you think Harry likes to scare people?

_____

_____

_____

_____

_____

_____

_____

READ: Chapter 3
"Harry's Triple Revenge"

☆ **Strategy:** Find the Main Idea

Focus: As you read, use a sticky note to mark where Harry gets revenge. Page _____

 Respond: Reread page 33. What did Harry do to make Sidney run away screaming?

_____

_____

_____

_____

_____

_____

_____

Judy Moody Was in a Mood. **Not a Good Mood. A Bad Mood**

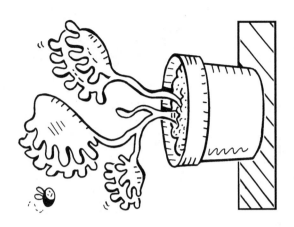

by Megan McDonald

Name _____

Date _____

SECTION 5

READ: **"The Me Collage" and "Band-Aids and Ice Cream"**

Strategy: Evaluate

Focus: As you read the first of these chapters, use a sticky note to mark where Judy has a big problem. Page _____

Respond: How has Judy changed since the beginning of the story?

_____
_____
_____
_____
_____
_____
_____
_____

SECTION 4

READ: **"The Worst Thing Ever," "Definitely the Worst Thing Ever," and "The Funniest Thing Ever"**

Strategy: Find the Main Idea

Focus: As you read the first of these chapters, use a sticky note to mark what Judy thought was the worst thing ever. Page _____

Respond: What was the funniest thing ever? What made it so funny?

_____
_____
_____
_____
_____
_____
_____
_____

READ: "A Bad Mood" and "Roar!"

 Strategy: Analyze Cause and Effect

 Focus: As you read the first of these chapters, use a sticky note to mark the reason Judy was in such a bad mood. Page _____

 Respond: How does Judy's opinion of third grade change after her first day of school? What makes her change her mind?

_____
_____
_____
_____
_____
_____
_____
_____

READ: "Two Heads Are Better Than One" and "My Favorite Pet"

Strategy: Question

Focus: As you read the first of these chapters, use a sticky note to mark the place where Stink outsmarts Judy. Page _____

Respond: What new pet does Judy get? Why do you think she chooses this pet?

_____
_____
_____
_____
_____
_____
_____
_____

READ: "My Smelly Pet," "Doctor Judy Moody," and "The T.P. Club"

Strategy: Make Inferences

Focus: As you read the first of these chapters, use a sticky note to mark the place that explains why Judy's backpack smells. Page _____

 **Respond:** What is the T.P. Club? Why does Stink want to be in the club?

_____
_____
_____
_____
_____
_____
_____
_____

ROSCOE RILEY RULES: Never Glue Your Friends to Chairs

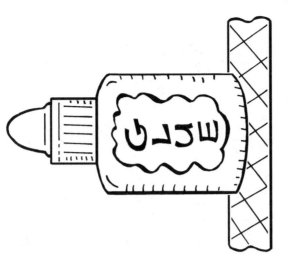

by Katherine Applegate

Name _____

Date _____

READ: CHAPTERS 11–13

★ **Strategy:** Evaluate

🔍 **Focus:** As you read, use a sticky note to mark something funny.

Page _____

✏️ **Respond:** What was your opinion of the story? Explain why you did or did not enjoy it.

_____
_____
_____
_____
_____
_____
_____
_____

READ: CHAPTERS 9 AND 10

★ **Strategy:** Predict

🔍 **Focus:** After reading Chapter 9, stop and write a prediction about what you think will happen in Chapter 10.

_____

 **Respond:** What did Roscoe do in Chapter 10? What do you think will happen to him as a result?

_____
_____
_____
_____
_____
_____

Reading Response Trifolds for 40 Favorite Chapter Books © Jennifer Cerra-Johansson Scholastic Teaching Resources • page 23

Strategy: Question

 Focus: What question came into your mind while previewing the cover, title, and illustrations?

If your question is answered in this section, mark it with a sticky note. Page ___

 Respond: On page 15 Roscoe says, "That's when all my trouble started." What trouble do you think Roscoe will have?

_____

_____

_____

_____

_____

_____

Strategy: Make Connections

 Focus: As you read Chapter 5, use a sticky note to mark a connection you made to the story. Page ___

Respond: How is Roscoe's school experience similar to yours?

_____

_____

_____

_____

_____

_____

Strategy: Find the Main Idea

Focus: As you read Chapter 7, use a sticky note to mark the place that explains why it is called "Mess Rehearsal." Page ___

Respond: What is Roscoe worried about at the end of Chapter 8?

_____

_____

_____

_____

_____

_____

Arthur's Mystery Envelope

by Marc Brown

Name _____

Date _____

Strategy: Find the Main Idea

 Focus: As you read Chapter 9, use a sticky note to mark where you found out what was inside the envelope. Page _____

Respond: What did Arthur learn from his experience with the "mystery envelope"?

Strategy: Make Inferences

 Focus: As you read Chapter 7, use a sticky note to mark a place that shows Arthur is feeling guilty. Page _____

 Respond: What is really happening on pages 45, 46, 47, and 48?

⭐ **Strategy:** Make Connections

🔍 **Focus:** As you read Chapter 1, use a sticky note to mark a place where you made a connection to the story. Page _____

✏️ **Respond:** How is Arthur feeling at the end of Chapter 2? Why? Have you ever felt this way?

⭐ **Strategy:** Evaluate

🔍 **Focus:** As you read Chapter 3, use a sticky note to mark the place where Arthur gets good advice from a friend. Page _____

 Respond: What do you think Arthur should do with the envelope? Why?

⭐ **Strategy:** Predict

🔍 **Focus:** As you read Chapter 5, use a sticky note to mark the place where something unexpected happens to the envelope. Page _____

 Respond: What do you think might happen if Arthur doesn't tell his parents about the envelope?

The Class Trip From the Black Lagoon

by Mike Thaler

Name _____

Date _____

SECTION 5

READ: Chapters 9–11

 Strategy: Make Inferences

Focus: As you read, use a sticky note to mark where the author uses a pun to make a joke.
Page _____

 Respond: Did the class actually go to a jungle? Where did they really go on their class trip?

_____
_____
_____
_____
_____
_____
_____
_____
_____
_____

SECTION 4

READ: Chapters 7 and 8

 Strategy: Predict

Focus: As you read Chapter 7, use a sticky note to mark where the author makes a joke.
Page _____

 Respond: Predict what you think will happen to the class in the jungle.

_____
_____
_____
_____
_____
_____
_____
_____
_____
_____

Strategy: Predict

Focus: Who do you think is telling the story, a character or a narrator?

_____

Respond: Predict where you think the class will go on the field trip.

Strategy: Question

Focus: As you read Chapter 3, use a sticky note to mark a place where you thought of a question. Page _____

Respond: On page 24, what is meant by "closet-ra-phobia"?

As you read Chapter 1, use a sticky note to mark a place where you find out. Page _____

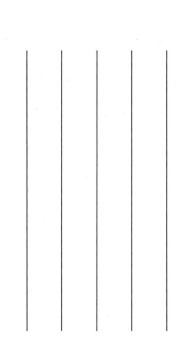

Strategy: Evaluate

Focus: As you read Chapter 5, use a sticky note to mark something funny. Page _____

Respond: Why do you think the author named the bus driver Mr. Fenderbender? What is a fenderbender?

Freckle Juice

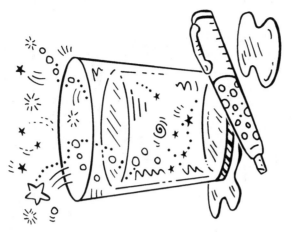

by Judy Blume

Name _____

Date _____

READ: Chapter 5

Strategy: Find the Main Idea

Focus: As you read, use a sticky note to mark the place where Andrew does something to show Sharon she didn't get the best of him. Page _____

Respond: What lesson does Andrew learn from Miss Kelly and the whole freckle-juice experience?

_____
_____
_____
_____
_____
_____
_____

READ: Chapter 4

Strategy: Predict

Focus: As you read, use a sticky note to mark the place where you discover if the recipe has worked. Page _____

Respond: What do you think Andrew will do to get back at Sharon?

_____
_____
_____
_____
_____
_____
_____

Strategy: Make Connections

 Focus: As you read, use a sticky note to mark a place where you made a personal connection to the story. Page ——

 **Respond:** How does Andrew feel about freckles? Have you ever felt this way about something?

——————————————
——————————————
——————————————
——————————————
——————————————
——————————————
——————————————
——————————————
——————————————
——————————————

Strategy: Evaluate

Focus: As you read, use a sticky note to mark the place where Andrew makes a decision about buying the freckle juice. Page ——

 Respond: Do you think Andrew should believe Sharon about the freckle juice recipe? Why or why not?

——————————————
——————————————
——————————————
——————————————
——————————————
——————————————
——————————————
——————————————
——————————————

Strategy: Predict

Focus: What do you think will be in the freckle juice recipe?

As you read, use a sticky note to mark the place where you find out. Page ——

 Respond: Do you think the recipe will work? Explain your answer.

——————————————
——————————————
——————————————
——————————————
——————————————
——————————————
——————————————
——————————————

Ivy and Bean

by Annie Barrows

Name _____

Date _____

READ: "The Spell" and "No Dessert"

⭐ **Strategy:** Evaluate

 **Focus:** As you read the first chapter, use a sticky note to mark a place that shows Ivy and Bean have become friends. Page _____

 Respond: What did you learn about friendship from reading this book?

READ: "Easy-Peasy" and "Bean's Backyard"

⭐ **Strategy:** Make Inferences

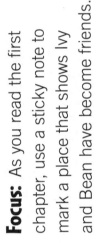 **Focus:** As you read the first chapter, use a sticky note to mark where Ivy does something surprising. Page _____

 Respond: How does Bean feel when she realizes Nancy is crying about getting her ears pierced? Why does she feel this way?

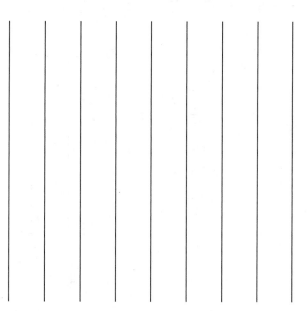

READ: "No Thanks" and "Bean Hatches a Plan"

☆ **Strategy:** Predict

Focus: Look at the cover and flip through the book. Predict what you think will happen in the story.

Respond: Predict what you think Bean will do to get back at her sister, Nancy.

READ: "The Ghost of Pancake Court" and "Bean Meets Ivy"

☆ **Strategy:** Make Connections

Focus: As you read the first of these chapters, use a sticky note to mark a place where you made a connection. Page _____

Respond: In "Bean Meets Ivy," how does Ivy surprise Bean? Write about a time when someone turned out to be different than you expected.

READ: "Ivy Hatches a Plan" and "Beware"

☆ **Strategy:** Find the Main Idea

Focus: As you read the first chapter, use a sticky note to mark the place where Bean thinks of a new plan to get back at Nancy. Page _____

Respond: In "Beware," how does Bean's opinion of Ivy change?

Katie Kazoo, Switcheroo: Anyone But Me

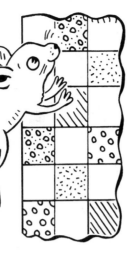

by Nancy Krulik

Name _____

Date _____

SECTION 5

READ: Chapters 9 and 10

⭐ **Strategy:** Evaluate

🔍 **Focus:** As you read Chapter 9, use a sticky note to mark a place that shows George has changed. Page _____

✏️ **Respond:** What did Katie learn about bullies?

SECTION 4

READ: Chapters 7 and 8

⭐ **Strategy:** Make Inferences

🔍 **Focus:** As you read Chapter 7, use a sticky note to mark a place where George seems scared. Page _____

✏️ **Respond:** Describe George's behavior in Chapter 8. Why is he acting this way?

⭐ **Strategy:** Make Connections

🔍 **Focus:** As you read Chapter 1, use a sticky note to mark a place where you made connection to the story. Page ____

✏️ **Respond:** What did Katie do on page 12 that embarrassed her in front of her class? Write about a time you felt this way.

_____
_____
_____
_____
_____
_____
_____
_____
_____

⭐ **Strategy:** Find the Main Idea

🔍 **Focus:** As you read Chapter 3, use a sticky note to mark where Katie makes a wish. Page ____

✏️ **Respond:** What happens to Katie in Chapter 4? What do you think caused her transformation?

_____
_____
_____
_____
_____
_____
_____
_____
_____

⭐ **Strategy:** Predict

🔍 **Focus:** Predict how Katie will escape.

 As you read Chapter 5, use a sticky note to mark where you find out how she escapes. Page ____

 Respond: Where do you think Katie will go after escaping the cage?

_____
_____
_____
_____
_____
_____
_____
_____
_____

The Magic Tree House: Dinosaurs Before Dark

by Mary Pope Osborne

Name _____

Date _____

SECTION 5

READ: Chapters 9 and 10

Strategy: Analyze Cause and Effect

Focus: As you read Chapter 9, use a sticky note to mark where Jack gets them back to Frog Creek. Page _____

Respond: Reread page 64. What caused the tree house to take Jack and Annie back in time?

SECTION 4

READ: Chapters 7 and 8

Strategy: Make Inferences

Focus: As you read Chapter 7, use a sticky note to mark the place where Jack does something brave. Page _____

Respond: Reread the first paragraph on page 52. What is Annie trying to tell the Pteranodon?

☆ **Strategy:** Predict

🔍 **Focus:** Before reading, predict the setting of the story.

✏️ **Respond:** As you read Chapter 1, use a sticky note to mark evidence of the setting. Page ____

Predict where you think the tree house has taken Jack and Annie. Explain your reasoning.

_____
_____
_____
_____
_____
_____
_____

 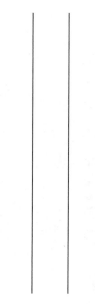

☆ **Strategy:** Find the Main Idea

🔍 **Focus:** As you read Chapter 3, use a sticky note to mark where the tree house has taken Jack and Annie. Page ____

✏️ **Respond:** Who is Henry?

_____
_____
_____
_____
_____
_____
_____

☆ **Strategy:** Question

🔍 **Focus:** As you read Chapter 5, use a sticky note to mark the place where Jack makes a discovery. Page ____

✏️ **Respond:** Why do the Anatosauruses run away on page 40?

_____
_____
_____
_____
_____
_____
_____

Miss Daisy Is Crazy

by Dan Gutman

Name _____

Date _____

Strategy: Evaluate

Focus: As you read, use a sticky note to mark where AJ learns a lesson from someone famous.
Page _____

Respond: What was Miss Daisy trying to teach AJ about learning and school?

_____
_____
_____
_____
_____
_____
_____
_____

Strategy: Analyze Cause and Effect

Focus: As you read, use a sticky note to mark a place where Miss Daisy tricks AJ into learning.
Page _____

Respond: How is the video game idea affecting the students who attend AJ's school?

_____
_____
_____
_____
_____
_____
_____
_____

☆ **Strategy:** Predict

🔍 **Focus:** Where do you think this story will take place?

 As you read Chapter 1, use a sticky note to mark evidence of the story's setting. Page _____

✏️ **Respond:** On page 9, Miss Daisy says she doesn't understand arithmetic. Predict whether or not she's telling the truth. Explain your prediction.

☆ **Strategy:** Question

🔍 **Focus:** As you read Chapter 3, use a sticky note to mark something surprising. Page _____

✏️ **Respond:** Who does AJ suspect Miss Daisy really is? Why does he think this?

☆ **Strategy:** Make Connections

🔍 **Focus:** As you read Chapter 5, use a sticky note to mark a place where you made a connection to the story. Page _____

 ✏️ **Respond:** What does AJ want to be when he grows up? What do you want to be?

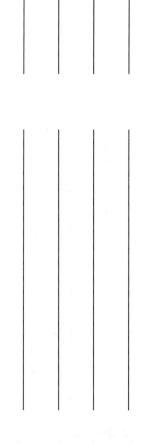

A to Z Mysteries: The Absent Author

by Ron Roy

Name _____

Date _____

SECTION 5   READ: Chapters 9 and 10

Strategy: Find the Main Idea

Focus: As you read Chapter 9, use a sticky note to mark an unexpected event. Page _____

Respond: What clues helped Ruth Rose solve the mystery?

_____
_____
_____
_____
_____
_____
_____
_____
_____
_____
_____

SECTION 4   READ: Chapters 7 and 8

Strategy: Predict

Focus: As you read Chapter 7, use a sticky note to mark where the kids learn something new about Wallis Wallace.

Respond: What do you think the kids will find when they open the door to room 302?

_____
_____
_____
_____
_____
_____
_____
_____
_____
_____
_____

Strategy: Predict

Focus: As you read Chapter 1, use a sticky note to mark the reason Dink is excited.
Page ____

Respond: What does Dink predict happened to Wallis Wallace? Why?

_____
_____
_____
_____
_____
_____
_____
_____
_____
_____

Strategy: Find the Main Idea

Focus: As you read Chapter 3, use a sticky note to mark where Dink gets something useful that could help the kids find Wallis Wallace. Page ____

Respond: What do the kids learn about Wallis Wallace in Chapter 4?

_____
_____
_____
_____
_____
_____
_____
_____
_____
_____

Strategy: Question

Focus: As you read Chapter 5, use a sticky note to mark a place where you thought of a question. Page ____

Respond: What did the kids learn on page 51? What did it lead them to believe?

_____
_____
_____
_____
_____
_____
_____
_____
_____
_____

Amber Brown Is Not a Crayon

by Paula Danziger

Name _____

Date _____

 Strategy: Evaluate

 **Focus:** As you read Chapter 8, use a sticky note to mark a place where Amber's feelings have changed. Page ____

Respond: What does Amber learn about friendship?

_____

_____

_____

_____

_____

_____

_____

_____

_____

_____

 Strategy: Predict

Focus: As you read Chapter 6, use a sticky note to mark evidence of Amber's feelings. Page ____

 Respond: What happens at the end of Chapter 7? Predict what you think will happen with Amber and Justin's friendship.

_____

_____

_____

_____

_____

_____

_____

_____

READ: Chapter 1

 Strategy: Find the Main Idea

 Focus: As you read, use a sticky note to mark a place that shows who is telling the story.

Page ____

Is it a character or a narrator?

 Respond: What did you learn about Amber and her personality from reading this chapter? Name at least three things.

READ: Chapters 2 and 3

 Strategy: Make Inferences

Focus: As you read Chapter 2, use a sticky note to mark an example of something that upsets Amber. Page ____

 Respond: Reread page 28. Why does Amber say there are "alligators in the toilet"?

READ: Chapters 4 and 5

 Strategy: Make Connections

Focus: As you read Chapter 4, use a sticky note to mark the place where Justin and Amber get a surprise. Page ____

 Respond: How is Amber feeling in Chapter 5? Write about a time you felt this way.

Be a Perfect Person in Just Three Days

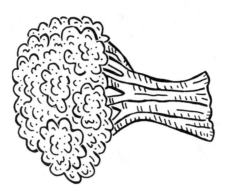

by **Stephen Manes**

Name _____

Date _____

Strategy: Evaluate

Focus: As you read Chapter 5, use a sticky note to mark where Milo fails at being perfect. Page _____

Respond: What does Milo learn from Dr. Silverfish?

_____
_____
_____
_____
_____
_____
_____
_____

Strategy: Question

Focus: As you read, use a sticky note to mark where Milo finds out what he needs to do on the second day. Page _____

Respond: How will going a whole day without food make Milo perfect?

_____
_____
_____
_____
_____
_____
_____

⭐ **Strategy:** Predict

🔍 **Focus:** Look at the first picture in the story. Predict what you think might happen in this chapter.

✏️ **Respond:** Do you think Milo will become perfect? Why or why not?

_____

_____

_____

_____

_____

_____

_____

⭐ **Strategy:** Make Connections

🔍 **Focus:** As you read, use a sticky note to mark a place where you made a connection. Page _____

✏️ **Respond:** Reread page 19. How does Milo feel about the way his family treats him? Do you ever feel this way? Explain your answer.

_____

_____

_____

_____

_____

_____

_____

⭐ **Strategy:** Use Context Clues

🔍 **Focus:** As you read, stop at the pages below and write what you think each word means.

Page	Word	I think it means . . .
29	dawdled	
30	inquired	
32	consumption	
35	futile	
36	pungent	

✏️ **Respond:** On page 36, Milo ignored his sister's "snide remarks about the broccoli." What does the author mean by this?

_____

_____

_____

_____

CATWINGS

by Ursula K. Le Guin

Name _____

Date _____

SECTION 5   **AFTER READING**

⭐ **Strategy:** Evaluate

✏️ **Respond:** What was your favorite part of the story? Why?

_____
_____
_____
_____
_____
_____
_____
_____
_____
_____
_____
_____

SECTION 4   **READ: Chapter 4**

Strategy: Find the Main Idea

 Focus: As you read, use a sticky note to mark something good that happens to the Tabbies.

Page _____

✏️ **Respond:** How does life change for the Tabbies in Chapter 4?

_____
_____
_____
_____
_____
_____
_____
_____

Strategy: Predict

Focus: Based on the cover and title, predict what you think will happen in the story.

Respond: Where do you think the Tabbies will go?

_____
_____
_____
_____
_____
_____
_____
_____
_____
_____
_____

Strategy: Use Context Clues

Focus: As you read, stop at the pages below and write what you think each word means.

Page	Word	I think it means . . .
12	pinnacle	_____
12	ease	_____
11	steeple	_____
15	descended	_____
15	pavement	_____

Respond: How is the Tabbies' new home different from the old "alley"?

_____
_____
_____
_____
_____
_____
_____

Strategy: Make Inferences

Focus: As you read, use a sticky note to mark a place where one of the Tabbies shows bravery.

Page _____

Respond: Why did owl try to hurt the Tabbies?

_____
_____
_____
_____
_____
_____
_____

The Chocolate Touch

by Patrick Skene Catling

Name _____

Date _____

SECTION 5   READ: Chapters 10–12

 Strategy: Evaluate

 Focus: As you read, use a sticky note to mark the place where John shows he has changed. Page ____

 Respond: What do you think is the moral of this story?

_____

_____

_____

_____

_____

_____

_____

_____

_____

_____

SECTION 4   READ: Chapters 8 and 9

 **Strategy:** Predict

 Focus: As you read Chapter 8, use a sticky note to mark a place where you made a prediction. Page ____

 Respond: What do you think John will do to solve his chocolate problem?

_____

_____

_____

_____

_____

_____

_____

_____

_____

_____

READ: Chapters 1 and 2

⭐ **Strategy:** Predict

🔍 **Focus:** Why do you think there is a sketch of a chocolate bar on the first page? As you read Chapter 1, use a sticky note to mark the place where you learn how the chocolate relates to John's problem. Page ____

 Respond: Predict what you think will happen when John wakes up the next morning.

____
____
____
____
____
____

READ: Chapters 3–5

⭐ **Strategy:** Analyze Cause and Effect

🔍 **Focus:** As you read, use a sticky note to mark an example of how John affects objects he puts in his mouth. Page ____

 Respond: How has John changed? What do you think caused this change?

____
____
____
____
____
____
____

READ: Chapters 6 and 7

⭐ **Strategy:** Find the Main Idea

🔍 **Read: Focus:** As you read Chapter 6, use a sticky note to mark an example of something bad happening to John. Page ____

 Respond: How is John feeling at the end of Chapter 8? Why is he feeling this way?

____
____
____
____
____
____

Donavan's Word Jar

by Monalisa DeGross

Name _____

Date _____

SECTION 5

READ: Chapters 9 and 10

Strategy: Evaluate

Focus: As you read Chapter 9, use a sticky note to mark where Donavan uses his word jar to solve a problem. Page _____

Respond: What did Donavan learn about the power of words?

_____
_____
_____
_____
_____
_____
_____
_____
_____
_____

SECTION 4

READ: Chapters 7 and 8

Strategy: Make Connections

Focus: As you read Chapter 7, use a sticky note to mark a place where you made a connection to the story. Page _____

Respond: What was Grandma's idea? Whom do you ask for advice when you have a problem?

_____
_____
_____
_____
_____
_____
_____
_____
_____
_____

⭐ **Strategy:** Find the Main Idea

🔍 **Focus:** As you read Chapter 1, use a sticky note to mark where you learn what Donavan collects.

Page ____

✏️ **Respond:** How did Donavan's interest in words begin?

_____
_____
_____
_____
_____
_____
_____
_____
_____
_____
_____
_____

⭐ **Strategy:** Make Inferences

 Focus: As you read Chapter 3, use a sticky note to mark Donavan's problem.

Page ____

✏️ **Respond:** Why is Donavan so anxious to visit his grandmother?

_____
_____
_____
_____
_____
_____
_____
_____
_____
_____
_____

⭐ **Strategy:** Predict

 Focus: Before reading Chapter 5, predict whether or not you think Donavan will stay home as his mother has told him to do.

✏️ **Respond:** Do you think Donavan's grandmother will help him solve his problem? Why or why not?

_____
_____
_____
_____
_____
_____
_____
_____
_____
_____

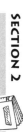
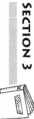

FLAT Stanley

by Jeff Brown

Name _____

Date _____

READ: Chapter 5

⭐ **Strategy:** Evaluate

🔍 **Focus:** Using a sticky note, mark a place where an important change takes place.
Page _____

✏️ **Respond:** What is one lesson you think Stanley learned from his "flat" experience?

READ: Chapter 4

⭐ **Strategy:** Identify the Main Idea

🔍 **Focus:** Using a sticky note, mark a place where Stanley does something heroic.
Page _____

✏️ **Respond:** Why is Chapter 4 called "The Museum Thieves"?

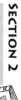

★ **Strategy:** Predict

🔍 **Focus:** Before reading, look at the cover. How do you think Stanley will become flat?

_____
_____
_____
_____
_____

✏️ **Respond:** How do you think Stanley's life will change now that he is flat?

_____
_____
_____
_____
_____

★ **Strategy:** Make Connections

🔍 **Focus:** Using a sticky note, mark an example of something exciting Stanley does in this chapter. Page _____

✏️ **Respond:** If you could be Stanley, what experience from this chapter would you most enjoy? Why?

_____
_____
_____
_____
_____

As you read, use a sticky note to mark the place where you find out. Page _____

★ **Strategy:** Use Context Clues

🔍 **Focus:** As you read, use the clues in the story to help you guess the meaning of the words below.

Page	Word	I think it means . . .
23	jostled	_____
24	parcel	_____
30	trousers	_____
33	cross	_____
33	phases	_____

✏️ **Respond:** On page 33, Mr. Lambchop says, "Kids are like that" and they go through "phases." What does he mean?

_____
_____
_____
_____
_____

The Gadget War

by Betsy Duffey

Name _____

Date _____

Strategy: Evaluate

Focus: As you read, use a sticky note to mark where Kelly does something brave. Page ____

Respond: What did Kelly learn from the "gadget war" with Albert?

_____

_____

_____

_____

_____

_____

_____

Strategy: Predict

Focus: As you read Chapter 8, use a sticky note to mark a place where you made a prediction. Page ____

Respond: Do you think Mr. Hardeman will find out that it was Kelly who threw the orange? What do you think will happen next?

_____

_____

_____

_____

_____

_____

_____

Strategy: Predict

Focus: As you read Chapter 1, use a sticky note to mark Kelly's problem. Page _____

Respond: Predict what you think will happen between Kelly and Albert.

_____
_____
_____
_____
_____
_____
_____
_____
_____
_____
_____
_____

Strategy: Find the Main Idea

Focus: As you read, use a sticky note to mark where Kelly gets an idea that could solve her problem. Page _____

Respond: What does Kelly invent? How will this help her with Albert Jones?

_____
_____
_____
_____
_____
_____
_____
_____
_____
_____
_____
_____
_____
_____

Strategy: Make Connections

Focus: As you read Chapter 6, use a sticky note to mark a place where you made a connection to the story. Page _____

Respond: Reread page 43. How does Kelly feel when Albert puts his head down? How would you have felt if you were Kelly? Why?

Jigsaw Jones: The Case of Hermie the Missing Hamster

by James Preller

Name _____

Date _____

READ: Chapters 11 and 12

☆ **Strategy:** Find the Main Idea

🔍 **Focus:** As you read Chapter 11, use a sticky note to mark where Jigsaw solves the mystery.
Page _____

✏️ **Respond:** What surprise does the class get on page 72?

_____
_____
_____
_____
_____
_____
_____
_____

READ: Chapters 9 and 10

☆ **Strategy:** Question

🔍 **Focus:** As you read Chapter 9, use a sticky note to mark the place that shows why it is called "The Phony Clue." Page _____

 Respond: Why does Wingnut's mother scream on page 62?

_____
_____
_____
_____
_____
_____
_____
_____

READ: Chapters 1 and 2

Strategy: Find the Main Idea

Focus: As you read Chapter 1, use a sticky note to mark the problem in the story. Page ——

Respond: Who does Jigsaw suspect may have hurt Hermie?

_____

_____

_____

_____

_____

_____

_____

_____

_____

_____

_____

READ: Chapters 4 and 5

Strategy: Make Inferences

Focus: As you read Chapter 4, use a sticky note to mark a place where Jigsaw learns what snakes eat. Page ——

Respond: Reread page 31. Why does Mila look so worried?

_____

_____

_____

_____

_____

_____

_____

_____

_____

_____

_____

READ: Chapters 6–8

Strategy: Predict

Focus: After reading Chapter 6, predict what the kids will find in Jake's room.

As you read Chapter 7, use a sticky note to mark what the kids find. Page ——

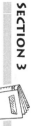

Respond: What does Jigsaw realize on page 50? Do you think he's right?

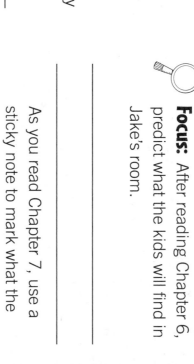

Lily and Miss Liberty

by Carla Stevens

Name _____

Date _____

SECTION 5

READ: Chapter Afterword

☆ **Strategy:** Evaluate

✏ **Respond:** What did the Statue of Liberty symbolize to Lily? What does "liberty" mean to you?

_____
_____
_____
_____
_____
_____
_____
_____
_____
_____

SECTION 4

READ: Chapters 6 and 7

☆ **Strategy:** Find the Main Idea

🔍 **Focus:** As you read Chapter 6, use a sticky note to mark the place where Lily gets a surprise. Page _____

✏ **Respond:** What happens to Lily on page 63?

_____
_____
_____
_____
_____
_____

 Strategy: Predict

 **Focus:** What do you think the setting of this story will be?

_____

As you read Chapter 1, use a sticky note to mark evidence of time and place. Page ____

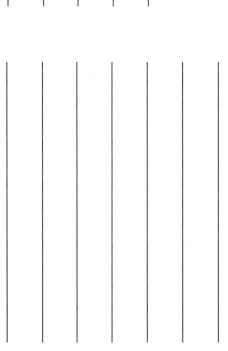 **Respond:** What is Lily's problem? How do you think she will solve it?

_____
_____
_____
_____
_____
_____
_____
_____
_____

Strategy: Make Inferences

Focus: As you read Chapter 3, use a sticky note to mark the place where Lily has an idea that might help her solve her problem. Page ____

 **Respond:** On page 28, Lily gives Rachel a free crown. Why does she do this?

_____
_____
_____
_____
_____
_____
_____
_____
_____

Strategy: Question

Focus: As you read, use a sticky note to mark where Lily does something kind. Page ____

 Respond: Why do you think Lily gives Lena the money?

_____
_____
_____
_____
_____
_____
_____
_____
_____

Ready Freddy: Tooth Trouble

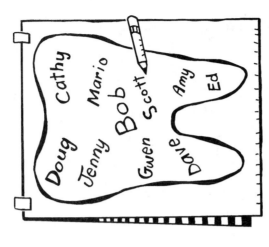

by Abby Klein

Name _____

Date _____

Strategy: Evaluate

 Focus: As you read, use a sticky note to mark a place where Freddy's sister Suzie helps him.
Page _____

 **Respond:** How did Freddy and Suzie's relationship change from the beginning to the end of the book?

_____
_____
_____
_____
_____
_____
_____

Strategy: Find the Main Idea

 Focus: As you read Chapter 7, use a sticky note to mark the place that explains the chapter title, "Hard, Crunchy Things."
Page _____

 **Respond:** How does Freddy's mom react to his fight at school? Why is Freddy surprised by her reaction?

_____
_____
_____
_____
_____
_____
_____

Strategy: Predict

Focus: Before reading, predict what you think Freddy's "tooth trouble" will be.

_____

As you read, use a sticky note to mark the place where you find out. Page ___

 Respond: Predict what you think Freddy's great idea will be.

_____

_____

_____

_____

_____

_____

_____

_____

Strategy: Make Connections

Focus: As you read Chapter 3, use a sticky note to mark a connection you made to the story. Page ___

Respond: How does Freddy feel about Max? Have you ever felt this way about a classmate? Explain.

_____

_____

_____

_____

_____

_____

_____

_____

_____

Strategy: Question

Focus: As you read Chapter 5, use a sticky note to mark where Freddy explains his plan to Robbie. Page ___

 Respond: Why didn't Freddy's plan work?

_____

_____

_____

_____

_____

_____

_____

_____

_____

The Secrets of Droon: The Hidden Stairs and the Magic Carpet

by Tony Abbott

Name _____

Date _____

SECTION 5

READ: Chapters 9 and 10

Strategy: Evaluate

Focus: As you read Chapter 9, use a sticky note to mark where Keeah does something clever.

Page _____

Respond: What was your favorite part of the story? Why?

_____
_____
_____
_____
_____
_____
_____
_____

SECTION 4

READ: Chapters 7 and 8

Strategy: Use Context Clues

Focus: As you read, stop at the pages below and write what you think each word means.

Page	Word	I think it means...
48	cloak	_____
50	reins	_____
52	grove	_____
54	peered	_____
59	raid	_____
64	narrow	_____

Respond: On page 65, Julie says, "We found a dungeon all by ourselves." What is a "dungeon"?

_____
_____
_____

READ: Chapters 1 and 2

Strategy: Predict

Focus: After reading Chapter 1, stop and make a prediction.

Respond: On page 15, an arrow shoots past the three kids. What do you think will happen in the next chapter?

_____

_____

_____

_____

_____

_____

_____

READ: Chapters 3 and 4

Strategy: Visualize

Focus: As you read Chapter 3, use a sticky note to mark a place you could visualize well.

Page ____

Respond: Reread page 26. Draw how you visualized Lord Sparr's "car" in your mind.

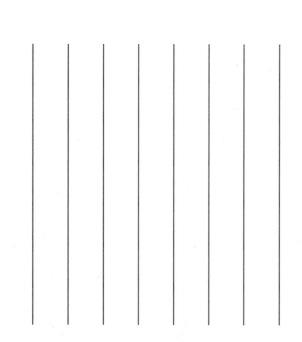

READ: Chapters 5 and 6

Strategy: Find the Main Idea

Focus: As you read Chapter 5, use a sticky note to mark who lives in the "vanishing tower."

Page ____

Respond: Why is Chapter 6 called "Home Must Wait"?

_____

_____

_____

_____

_____

_____

_____

The Stories Julian Tells

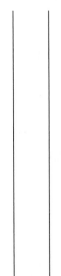

by Ann Cameron

Name _____

Date _____

SECTION 5

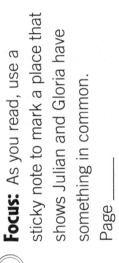

READ: "Gloria Who Might Be My Best Friend"

⭐ **Strategy:** Evaluate

🔍 **Focus:** As you read, use a sticky note to mark a place that shows Julian and Gloria have something in common.
Page _____

✏️ **Respond:** What does Gloria say on page 62 that makes Julian like her right away and want to become her friend? Would you have felt the same way as Julian? Why or why not?

_____

_____

_____

_____

_____

_____

_____

SECTION 4

READ: "My Very Strange Teeth"

⭐ **Strategy:** Make Connections

 Focus: As you read, use a sticky note to mark a place where you made a connection to the story.
Page _____

✏️ **Respond:** How did Julian's tooth eventually come out? Have you ever had a similar experience with a loose tooth? Explain.

_____

_____

_____

_____

_____

_____

Reading Response Trifolds for 40 Favorite Chapter Books © Jennifer Cerra-Johansson Scholastic Teaching Resources • page 63

READ: "The Pudding Like a Night on the Sea"

⭐ **Strategy:** Predict

🔍 **Focus:** As you read, use a sticky note to mark a place where you made a prediction. Page ____

✏️ **Respond:** What did Huey say on page 12 when his father asked if there was something the boys had to tell him? Do you think Huey and Julian will eventually confess to what they did? Why or why not?

READ: "Catalog Cats"

⭐ **Strategy:** Make Inferences

🔍 **Focus:** As you read, use a sticky note to mark where Julian fibs to his brother Huey. Page ____

✏️ **Respond:** Why doesn't Julian's dad tell Huey the truth about the catalog cats?

READ: "Our Garden" and "Because of Figs"

⭐ **Strategy:** Question

🔍 **Focus:** As you read the first of these chapters, use a sticky note to mark a place where you thought of a question. Page ____

✏️ **Respond:** Why didn't Julian tell his father about eating the fig tree's leaves?

Third-Grade Detectives:

The Clue of the Left-Handed Envelope

by George E. Stanley

Name _____

Date _____

Strategy: Evaluate

Focus: As you read Chapter 9, use a sticky note to mark where Noelle and Todd solve the mystery. Page _____

Respond: Why do you think Mr. Merlin spent so much class time helping the kids solve the mystery? What was he trying to teach them?

_____

Strategy: Make Inferences

Focus: As you read Chapter 7, use a sticky note to mark where the kids learned something important about the person who sent the envelope. Page _____

Respond: On page 48, Noelle notices Leon is left-handed. Why is this important?

_____

READ: Chapters 1 and 2

⭐ **Strategy:** Find the Main Idea

🔍 **Focus:** As you read Chapter 1, use a sticky note to mark where you learned the problem in the story. Page _____

✏️ **Respond:** What was the secret code clue?

_____

_____

_____

_____

_____

_____

_____

_____

READ: Chapters 3 and 4

⭐ **Strategy:** Question

🔍 **Focus:** As you read Chapter 3, use a sticky note to mark the second clue Mr. Merlin gives the class. Page _____

✏️ **Respond:** How do you think this clue will help the kids solve the mystery?

_____

_____

_____

_____

_____

_____

_____

_____

READ: Chapters 5 and 6

⭐ **Strategy:** Predict

🔍 **Focus:** Before reading Chapter 5, predict whether Amber Lee will have already solved the mystery.

As you read Chapter 5, use a sticky note to mark the place where you find out. Page _____

✏️ **Respond:** On the last page of Chapter 6, Noelle thinks she's discovered the importance of licking the envelope. Do you think she'll be right? Why or why not?

_____

_____

_____

_____

_____

_____

The Courage of Sarah Noble

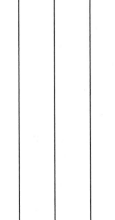

by Alice Dalgliesh

Name _____

Date _____

SECTION 5 **READ: Chapters 9–11**

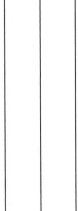 **Strategy:** Evaluate

 **Focus:** As you read, use a sticky note to mark an example of how Sarah has changed since the beginning of the story. Page _____

 **Respond:** What did Sarah learn from living with the Indians?

_____
_____
_____
_____
_____
_____
_____
_____
_____

SECTION 4 **READ: Chapters 7 and 8**

 Strategy: Make Connections

 Focus: As you read Chapter 7, use a sticky note to mark a place where you made a connection to the story. Page _____

 **Respond:** How does Sarah feel her first night with the Indians? How do you feel when you sleep away from home?

_____
_____
_____
_____
_____
_____
_____

⭐ **Strategy:** Predict

🔍 **Focus:** Before reading, predict where you think this story might take place.

✏️ **Respond:** Predict what you think will happen when Sarah and her father reach their new land.

As you read Chapter 1, use a sticky note to mark evidence of the setting. Page ____

⭐ **Strategy:** Visualize

🔍 **Focus:** As you read Chapter 3, use a sticky note to mark a place you could visualize well. Page ____

✏️ **Respond:** How did you visualize the cave in your mind? Draw it.

⭐ **Strategy:** Find the Main Idea

🔍 **Focus:** As you read Chapter 5, use a sticky note to mark a place where Sarah shows cleverness. Page ____

✏️ **Respond:** Why is Chapter 6 called "Friends"?

Gooney Bird Greene

by Lois Lowry

Name _____

Date _____

SECTION 5

READ: Chapters 6 and 7

⭐ **Strategy:** Find the Main Idea

🔍 **Focus:** As you read Chapter 6, use a sticky note to mark where you learn how Catman was consumed by a cow. Page _____

✏️ **Respond:** What did Gooney Bird teach her classmates about telling and writing stories?

_____
_____
_____
_____
_____
_____
_____
_____
_____

SECTION 4

READ: Chapter 5

⭐ **Strategy:** Make Inferences

🔍 **Focus:** As you read, use a sticky note to mark something that surprised you. Page _____

✏️ **Respond:** Was Gooney Bird's story about directing a band true? Do you think all her stories are true? Why or why not?

_____
_____
_____
_____
_____
_____
_____
_____
_____

READ: Chapters 1 and 2

Strategy: Predict

Focus: After reading Chapter 1, predict whether or not you think Gooney's story will be true.

_____
_____
_____
_____
_____

Respond: How did Gooney Bird get her name? Do you believe her story?

_____
_____
_____
_____
_____
_____
_____

READ: Chapter 3

Strategy: Use Context Clues

Focus: As you read, stop at the pages below and write what you think each word means.

Page	Word	I think it means . . .
22	satin	
25	constantly	
26	sternly	
26	intermission	
29	sentimental	
32	pothole	

Respond: On page 34, Gooney says her cat was "consumed by a cow." What does she mean?

_____
_____
_____
_____
_____

READ: Chapter 4

Strategy: Find the Main Idea

Focus: As you read, use a sticky note to mark where you learn how Gooney got her diamond earrings. Page _____

Respond: Who was the "Prince" and what was the "Palace"?

_____
_____
_____
_____
_____
_____
_____

The Hundred Dresses

by Eleanor Estes

Name _____

Date _____

SECTION 5

READ: Chapter 7

☆ **Strategy:** Evaluate

🔍 **Focus:** As you read, use a sticky note to mark a place that shows Maddie and Peggy have changed. Page _____

✏️ **Respond:** What is the moral or lesson the author wants you to learn from reading this story?

_____
_____
_____
_____
_____
_____
_____
_____

SECTION 4

READ: Chapter 6

☆ **Strategy:** Use Context Clues

🔍 **Focus:** As you read, stop at the pages below and write what you think each word means.

Page	Word	I think it means . . .
51	dismal	_____
52	assailed	_____
53	remnant	_____
54	sparse	_____
56	timidly	_____
59	dilapidated	_____
61	disconsolate	_____

 Respond: On page 63, Maddie "reached an important conclusion." What conclusion or decision did Maddie make?

_____
_____
_____

Strategy: Question

Focus: As you read Chapter 1, use a sticky note to mark a place where you learn something about Wanda. Page ____

Respond: Why do Peggy and the other girls keep asking Wanda about the hundred dresses?

Strategy: Make Inferences

Focus: As you read, use a sticky note to mark how the hundred dresses game began. Page ____

Respond: On page 24, why did Wanda want to stay behind with the group of girls instead of walking to school with her brother?

Strategy: Find the Main Idea

Focus: As you read Chapter 4, use a sticky note to mark the reason Maddie never stood up for Wanda. Page ____

Respond: What did you learn about the hundred dresses in Chapter 5?

Jake Drake
Know-It-All

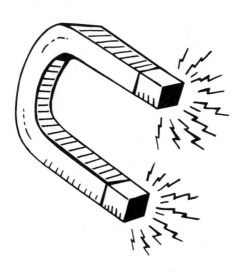

by Andrew Clements

Name _____

Date _____

READ: Chapters 10 and 11

Strategy: Evaluate

 Focus: As you read Chapter 10, use a sticky note to mark a place that shows Jake's new attitude toward the science fair. Page _____

Respond: What did Jake learn from his science fair experience?

_____
_____
_____
_____
_____
_____
_____

READ: Chapters 8 and 9

Strategy: Question

Focus: As you read Chapter 8, use a sticky note to mark where Jake makes a surprising decision. Page _____

 Respond: Why does Jake decide to become partners with Willie?

_____
_____
_____
_____
_____
_____
_____

⭐ **Strategy:** Make Connections

🔍 **Focus:** As you read Chapter 1, use a sticky note to mark a place where you made a connection. Page ___

✏️ **Respond:** Why did Jake want to win the science fair? Have you ever entered a contest? Write about it.

___

⭐ **Strategy:** Predict

🔍 **Focus:** As you read Chapters 3 and 4, use a sticky note to mark a place where you made a prediction. Page ___

✏️ **Respond:** What do you think Jake will do for the science fair?

___

⭐ **Strategy:** Find the Main Idea

🔍 **Focus:** As you read Chapter 6, use a sticky note to mark Jake's idea. Page ___

✏️ **Respond:** What does Chapter 7 show about Jake's personality and character?

Muggie Maggie

by Beverly Cleary

Name _____

Date _____

SECTION 5   READ: Chapter 8

⭐ **Strategy:** Evaluate

🔍 **Focus:** As you read, use a sticky note to mark a place that shows Maggie has changed. Page _____

✏️ **Respond:** Do you think it's important to learn cursive? Why or why not?

_____
_____
_____
_____
_____
_____
_____
_____
_____

SECTION 4   READ: Chapters 6 and 7

⭐ **Strategy:** Question

🔍 **Focus:** As you read Chapter 7, use a sticky note to mark where you discover the reason Mrs. Leeper made Maggie the "Message Monitor." Page _____

✏️ **Respond:** Why does Maggie practice cursive all weekend?

_____
_____
_____
_____
_____
_____
_____
_____
_____

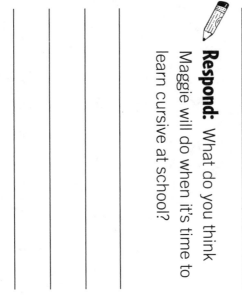

Strategy: Predict

Focus: Based on the cover, title, and illustrations in the book, predict what you think will happen.

✏️ **Respond:** What do you think Maggie will do when it's time to learn cursive at school?

_____
_____
_____
_____
_____
_____
_____
_____
_____
_____

Strategy: Use Context Clues

Focus: As you read, stop at the pages below and write what you think each word means.

Page	Word	I think it means . . .
14	demonstrate	_____
24	reluctant	_____
24	indignant	_____
25	dawdled	_____
28	grim	_____
29	suspicious	_____

✏️ **Respond:** On page 28, Maggie visits the school psychologist. What do you think a psychologist does?

_____
_____
_____
_____
_____
_____

Strategy: Make Connections

Focus: As you read Chapter 4, use a sticky note to mark a place where you made a connection to the story. Page _____

✏️ **Respond:** On page 41, what did Mrs. Madden ask Maggie in her letter? Would you have copied over the letter? Why or why not?

_____
_____
_____
_____
_____
_____
_____
_____

MY AMERICA: OUR STRANGE NEW LAND

by Patricia Hermes

Name _____

Date _____

SECTION 5 READ: Pages 84–98

Strategy: Evaluate

 Focus: As you read, use a sticky note to mark a happy event.
Page _____

Respond: How has Elizabeth's view of Jamestown changed since the beginning of the story?

_____

_____

_____

_____

_____

_____

_____

_____

_____

_____

_____

_____

SECTION 4 READ: Pages 64–83

Strategy: Predict

Focus: As you read, use a sticky note to mark where something bad happens to Captain Smith.
Page _____

Respond: Predict what you think will happen when Captain Smith leaves the Jamestown settlement.

_____

_____

_____

_____

_____

_____

_____

_____

_____

_____

READ: Pages 3–23

★ **Strategy:** Visualize

🔍 **Focus:** As you read, use a sticky note to mark evidence of when and where the story takes place.

Page ____

✏️ **Respond:** Reread the bottom half of page 9. Draw how you pictured the village in your mind after reading the author's description.

_____

_____

_____

READ: Pages 24–43

★ **Strategy:** Use Context Clues

🔍 **Focus:** As you read, stop at the pages below and write what you think each word means.

Page	Word	I think it means . . .
26	pallet	_____
28	toll	_____
33	mending	_____
35	strife	_____
41	weary	_____

✏️ **Respond:** On page 42, Elizabeth says her mama is not "fond" of the Bridger family. What does she mean by this?

_____

_____

_____

READ: Pages 44–63

★ **Strategy:** Analyze Cause and Effect

🔍 **Focus:** As you read, use a sticky note to mark where Elizabeth gets back at John Bridger for throwing a frog at her.

Page ____

✏️ **Respond:** In her September 18th entry on page 63, Elizabeth says that some of the men are leaving to start a new settlement. How do you think this will affect the colonists' relationship with the Native Americans living in the area?

Geronimo Stilton:
Lost Treasure of the Emerald Eye

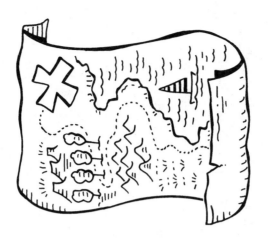

by Geronimo Stilton

Name _____

Date _____

SECTION 5

READ: Pages 96–116

⭐ **Strategy:** Find the Main Idea

🔍 **Focus:** As you read, use a sticky note to mark where Geronimo gets a surprise. Page ____

✏️ **Respond:** What was the treasure of the Emerald Eye?

_____
_____
_____
_____
_____
_____
_____
_____
_____
_____

SECTION 4

READ: Pages 72–95

⭐ **Strategy:** Use Context Clues

🔍 **Focus:** As you read, stop at the pages below and write what you think each word means.

Page	Word	I think it means . . .
72	regret	
74	provisions	
80	frantic	
86	clearing	
90	engraved	

✏️ **Respond:** On page 94, Trap "looked a little pale." What does "pale" mean in this sentence? What does this show about the way Trap is feeling?

_____
_____
_____

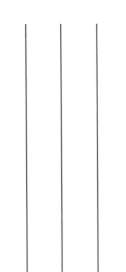

Strategy: Question

Focus: Preview the cover and illustrations. Write a question you thought of.

_____

_____

_____

When you find the answer to your question, mark it with a sticky note. Page _____

Respond: What is Thea's secret? Why does she want to keep it a secret?

_____

_____

_____

_____

_____

_____

_____

Strategy: Visualize

Focus: As you read, use a sticky note to mark a place you could visualize well. Page _____

Respond: Who is the mysterious passenger?

_____

_____

_____

_____

_____

_____

_____

_____

Strategy: Make Inferences

Focus: As you read, use a sticky note to mark where Geronimo learns something about Trap. Page _____

Respond: On page 65, why are the mice so happy when it rains?

_____

_____

_____

_____

_____

_____

_____

The Legend of Spud Murphy

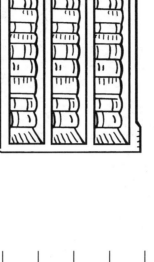

by Eoin Colfer

Name _____

Date _____

SECTION 5

READ: Chapter 5

Strategy: Evaluate

 Focus: As you read, use a sticky note to mark something that surprised you. Page _____

 Respond: What did Will learn by going to the library?

SECTION 4

READ: Chapter 4

Strategy: Find the Main Idea

Focus: As you read, use a sticky note to mark a place where Will does something new. Page _____

Respond: Why is Chapter 4 called "A Good Book"?

☆ **Strategy:** Predict

🔍 **Focus:** Predict who you think will tell the story.

✏️ **Respond:** Predict if you think the boys are telling the truth about Mrs. Murphy. Explain your prediction.

_____
_____
_____
_____
_____

Use a sticky note to mark where you find out. Page ____

☆ **Strategy:** Visualize

🔍 **Focus:** As you read, use a sticky note to mark a place you could visualize well. Page ____

✏️ **Respond:** Reread the bottom half of page 30. Draw how you visualized the junior section of the library.

☆ **Strategy:** Use Context Clues

🔍 **Focus:** As you read, stop at the pages below and write what you think each word means.

Page	Word	I think it means...
33	suspended	
34	hysterics	
36	mischief	
39	precise	
48	eternity	

✏️ **Respond:** On page 42, it says Marty knew he'd "met his match." What does Will mean by this?

_____
_____
_____
_____

26 Fairmount Avenue

by Tomie DePaola

Name _____

Date _____

SECTION 5 READ: Chapters 8 and 9

Strategy: Make Connections

Focus: As you read Chapter 8, use a sticky note to mark a connection you made to the story. Page _____

Respond: How does Tomie feel about moving into his new home? How would you feel if you moved into a new home? Have you ever moved? How did you feel?

_____
_____
_____
_____
_____
_____
_____
_____

SECTION 4 READ: Chapters 6 and 7

Strategy: Predict

Focus: After reading Chapter 6, make a prediction about what you think will happen next.

_____

Respond: Do you think Tomie's family will move into the house? Explain your prediction.

_____
_____
_____
_____
_____
_____
_____
_____

Strategy: Find the Main Idea

Focus: As you read, use a sticky note to mark something important that happens. Page ____

Respond: What would be a good title for Chapter 1? Explain your answer.

_____

_____

_____

_____

_____

_____

_____

_____

Strategy: Make Connections

Focus: As you read Chapter 2, use a sticky note to mark a connection you made to the story. Page ____

Respond: Why was Tomie so mad about the Snow White movie? Have you ever been disappointed by something you had been excited to see or do? Write about it.

_____

_____

_____

_____

_____

_____

_____

_____

Strategy: Question

Focus: As you read Chapter 4, use a sticky note to mark a question that came to your mind. Page ____

Respond: Why did Tomie leave kindergarten and walk home?

_____

_____

_____

_____

_____

_____

_____

_____

Yang the Youngest and His Terrible Ear

by Lensey Namioka

Name _____

Date _____

 Strategy: Evaluate

 **Focus:** As you read Chapter 7, use a sticky note to mark where Yangtao's father changes. Page _____

Respond: What is the moral of this story?

_____
_____
_____
_____
_____
_____
_____
_____
_____
_____

Strategy: Question

Focus: As you read, use a sticky note to mark where Yangtao's plan is ruined. Page _____

Respond: Why did Third Sister knock down the screen?

_____
_____
_____
_____
_____
_____
_____
_____
_____
_____

READ: Chapters 1 and 2

Strategy: Predict

Focus: Before reading, predict what you think Yang's problem will be.

As you read, use a sticky note to mark where you find out.

Page _____

Respond: After reading Chapter 2, predict what you think might happen in the story.

READ: Chapters 3 and 4

Strategy: Find the Main Idea

Focus: As you read Chapter 3, use a sticky note to mark where Yangtao learns something new from his friend. Page _____

Respond: How does Matthew's family feel about his friendship with Yangtao? Why?

READ: Chapter 5

Strategy: Make Inferences

Focus: As you read, use a sticky note to mark a place where you feel bad for one of the characters. Page _____

Respond: Reread the first half of page 81. Why does Mr. Conner remind Yangtao of his own father?

Bunnicula: A Rabbit-Tale of Mystery

by Deborah and James Howe

Name _____

Date _____

READ: Chapter 9

Strategy: Find the Main Idea

Focus: As you read, use a sticky note to mark where Bunnicula's problem is solved. Page _____

Respond: How does Harold's relationship with Bunnicula change from the beginning to the end of the story?

_____

_____

_____

_____

_____

_____

_____

READ: Chapters 7 and 8

Strategy: Analyze Cause and Effect

Focus: As you read Chapter 7, use a sticky note to mark where Chester's actions cause Bunnicula harm. Page _____

Respond: How does Harold try to help Bunnicula? How does this end up having a negative effect on Harold?

_____

_____

_____

_____

_____

_____

_____

☆ **Strategy:** Predict

🔍 **Focus:** Who do you think will tell this story?

✏ **Respond:** At the end of Chapter 2, what does Chester learn about Bunnicula? Predict what you think might happen in the next chapter.

☆ **Strategy:** Use Context Clues

🔍 **Focus:** As you read, stop at the pages below and write what you think each word means.

Page	Word	I think it means . . .
26	alert	
27	neglected	
30	tender	
30	incredulously	
35	significant	

✏ **Respond:** On page 51, Harold says his "throat contracted in fear." What does he mean by this? Why does he mention his throat?

☆ **Strategy:** Make Inferences

🔍 **Focus:** As you read Chapter 5, use a sticky note to mark where Chester feels embarrassed.

Page _____

✏ **Respond:** Reread page 72. What kind of sharp "stake" is the author talking about? What does Chester think the author means?

Charlotte's Web

by E.B. White

Name _____

Date _____

Strategy: Make Inferences

 Focus: As you read, use a sticky note to mark a place that shows Charlotte is changing. Page _____

 Respond: On page 164, what does Charlotte mean when she says, "By helping you, perhaps I was trying to lift my own life a trifle"?

_____
_____
_____
_____
_____
_____
_____

Strategy: Visualize

Focus: As you read, use a sticky note to mark a place where the author's description helps you visualize something clearly in your mind. Page _____

 Respond: Reread the last paragraph on page 136. Draw a picture of something you visualized while reading that paragraph.

Strategy: Predict

Focus: After reading Chapters 1 and 2, stop and make a prediction.

Was your prediction correct? As you read, use a sticky note to mark where you find out.

Page _____

Respond: Who do you think is speaking to Wilbur on page 31?

Strategy: Use Context Clues

Focus: As you read, stop at the pages below and write what you think each word means.

Page	Word	I think it means . . .
35	meekly	
37	near-sighted	
44	gratified	
47	lair	
54	queerly	
56	hastily	

Respond: On page 61, Charlotte explains that she is "sedentary." Do you think it's healthy for children to be sedentary? Why or why not?

Strategy: Make Connections

Focus: As you read, use a sticky note to mark a place where you made a connection to the story.

Page _____

Respond: In Chapter 13, what does Wilber ask Charlotte to do to help him fall asleep? What do you do when you have trouble falling asleep?

Name _____

Date _____

Title: _____

Author: _____

SECTION 4

READ: _____

Strategy: _____

Focus: _____

Respond: _____

SECTION 5

READ: _____

Strategy: _____

Focus: _____

Respond: _____

READ:

⭐ Strategy: _____

🔍 Focus: _____

✏️ Respond: _____

_____
_____
_____
_____
_____
_____
_____
_____
_____
_____
_____
_____

READ:

⭐ Strategy: _____

🔍 Focus: _____

✏️ Respond: _____

_____
_____
_____
_____
_____
_____
_____
_____
_____
_____
_____
_____

READ:

⭐ Strategy: _____

🔍 Focus: _____

✏️ Respond: _____

_____
_____
_____
_____
_____
_____
_____
_____
_____
_____
_____
_____

Name _____

Date _____

Title: _____

Author: _____

SECTION 4

READ: _____

⭐ **Strategy:** _____

🔍 **Focus:** _____
_____
_____

✏️ **Respond:** _____
_____
_____
_____
_____
_____
_____
_____

SECTION 5

READ: _____

⭐ **Strategy:** _____

🔍 **Focus:** _____
_____
_____

✏️ **Respond:** _____
_____
_____
_____
_____
_____
_____
_____

READ:

☆ Strategy: _____

🔍 Focus: _____

✏️ Respond: _____

_____
_____
_____
_____
_____
_____
_____
_____
_____

READ:

☆ Strategy: _____

🔍 Focus: _____

✏️ Respond: _____

_____
_____
_____
_____
_____
_____
_____
_____
_____

READ:

☆ Strategy: _____

🔍 Focus: _____

✏️ Respond: _____

_____
_____
_____
_____
_____
_____
_____
_____
_____

Bibliography

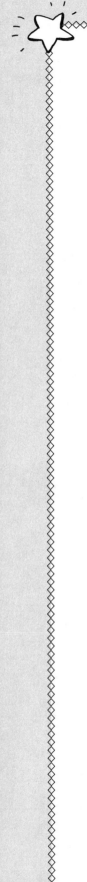

A to Z Mysteries: The Absent Author by Ron Roy (Random House, 1997)

Amber Brown Is Not a Crayon by Paula Danziger (Scholastic, 1994)

Amelia Bedelia by Peggy Parish (Scholastic, 1963)

Arthur's Mystery Envelope by Marc Browns (Little, Brown and Company, 1998)

Be a Perfect Person in Just Three Days by Stephen Manes (Dell, 1982)

Bunnicula: A Rabbit-Tale of Mystery by Deborah and James Howe (Aladdin, 1979)

Cam Jansen and the Mystery of the Stolen Diamonds by David A. Adler (Viking Press, 1980)

Catwings by Ursula K. LeGuin (Orchard Books, 1988)

Charlotte's Web by E.B. White (Scholastic, 1952)

The Chocolate Touch by Patrick Skene Catling (Yearling, 1952)

The Class Trip From the Black Lagoon by Mike Thaler (Scholastic, 2002)

The Cobble Street Cousins: In Aunt Lucy's Kitchen by Cynthia Rylant (Aladdin, 1998)

The Courage of Sarah Noble by Alice Dalgliesh (Aladdin, 1991)

Donavan's Word Jar by Monalisa DeGross (Scholastic, 1994)

Flat Stanley by Jeff Brown (Scholastic, 1964)

Freckle Juice by Judy Blume (Dell Yearling, 1971)

The Gadget War by Betsy Duffey (Puffin, 1991)

Geronimo Stilton: Lost Treasure of the Emerald Eye by Geronimo Stilton (Scholastic, 2004)

Gooney Bird Greene by Lois Lowry (Houghton Mifflin, 2002)

Horrible Harry in Room 2B by Suzy Kline (Puffin Book, 1988)

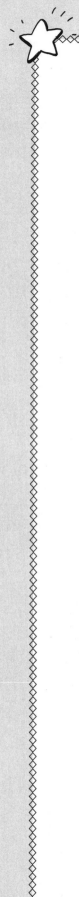

The Hundred Dresses by Eleanor Estes (Harcourt, 1944)

Ivy and Bean by Annie Barrows (Chronicle Books, 2006)

Jigsaw Jones: The Case of Hermie the Missing Hamster by James Preller (Scholastic, 1998)

Jake Drake Know-It-All by Andrew Clements (Aladdin, 2001)

Judy Moody Was in a Mood. Not a Good Mood. A Bad Mood. By Megan McDonald (Scholastic, 2000)

Katie Kazoo, Switcheroo: Anyone But Me by Nancy Krulik (Grosset and Dunlap, 2002)

The Legend of Spud Murphy by Eoin Colfer (Miramax, 2004)

Lily and Miss Liberty by Carla Stevens (Scholastic, 1992)

The Magic Tree House: Dinosaurs Before Dark (Scholastic, 1992)

Mercy Watson to the Rescue by Kate DiCamillo (Candlewick Press, 2009)

Miss Daisy Is Crazy by Dan Gutman (Scholastic, 2004)

Muggie Maggie by Beverly Cleary (Avon, 1990)

My America: Our Strange New Land by Patricia Hermes (Scholastic, 2000)

Ready Freddy: Tooth Trouble by Abby Klein (Scholastic, 2004)

Roscoe Riley Rules: Never Glue Your Friends to Chairs by Katherine Applegate (HarperTrophy, 2008)

The Secrets of Droon: The Hidden Stairs and the Magic Carpet by Tony Abbott (Scholastic, 1999)

The Stories Julian Tells by Ann Cameron (Alfred A. Knopf, 1981)

Third-Grade Detectives: The Clue of the Left-Handed Envelope by George E. Stanley (Scholastic, 2002)

26 Fairmount Avenue by Tomie DePaola (Scholastic, 1999)

Yang the Youngest and His Terrible Ear by Lensey Namioka (Dell, 1992)